After Fukushima

After Fukushima

The Equivalence of Catastrophes

JEAN-LUC NANCY

TRANSLATED BY CHARLOTTE MANDELL

FORDHAM UNIVERSITY PRESS
New York ✦ *2015*

This book was originally published in French as Jean-Luc Nancy, *L'Équivalence des catastrophes (Après Fukushima)* © Éditions Galilée, 2012.

Fordham University Press has no responsibility for the persistence or accuracy of URLs for external or third-party Internet websites referred to in this publication and does not guarantee that any content on such websites is, or will remain, accurate or appropriate.

Fordham University Press also publishes its books in a variety of electronic formats. Some content that appears in print may not be available in electronic books.

Library of Congress Cataloging-in-Publication Data

Nancy, Jean-Luc.
  [Équivalence des catastrophes (après Fukushima)]
  After Fukushima : the equivalence of catastrophes / Jean-Luc Nancy ; translated by Charlotte Mandell.
    pages cm
  Translation of: Équivalence des catastrophes (après Fukushima)
  Includes bibliographical references.
  ISBN 978-0-8232-6338-7 (hardback) — ISBN 978-0-8232-6339-4 (paper)
  1. Disasters—Philosophy. 2. Technology—Philosophy. 3. Fukushima Nuclear Disaster, Japan, 2011. I. Title.
  B2430.N363E6413 2015
  363.3401—dc23

                                                            2014027974

Printed in the United States of America

17 16 15   5 4 3 2 1

First edition

Contents

His heart,
in childhood, always delighted
in every leaf, every slice of sky,
contemplating his village. This future
was unaware that today
the horizon aligns itself with other
indifferences. Everything has happened:
in us, by fate,
we are prisoners of regret
for our innocence.

—Pier Paolo Pasolini, "Europa"

After Fukushima: The Equivalence of Catastrophes

Preamble

The subtitle should not mislead: Not all catastrophes are equivalent, not in amplitude, not in destructiveness, not in consequences. A tsunami without repercussions for a nuclear installation is not the same as a tsunami that seriously damages a nuclear plant. Negligence in managing this plant opens up yet another register of gravity.

Nuclear catastrophe—all differences military or civilian kept in mind—remains the one potentially irremediable catastrophe, whose effects spread through generations, through the layers of the earth; these effects have an impact on all living things and on the large-scale organization of energy production, hence on consumption as well.

The "equivalence" of catastrophes here means to assert that the spread or proliferation of repercussions from every kind of disaster hereafter will bear the mark of that paradigm represented by nuclear risk. From now on there is an interconnection, an intertwining, even a symbiosis of technologies, exchanges, movements, which makes it so that a flood—for instance—wherever it may occur, must necessarily involve relationships with any number of technical, social, economic, political intricacies that keep us from regarding it as simply a misadventure or a misfortune whose consequences can be more or less easily circumscribed. This is even truer for a chemical catastrophe such as the one in Bhopal in 1984,[1] the human, economic, and ecological effects of which are still visible today.

The complexity here is singularly characterized by the fact that natural catastrophes are no longer separable from their technological, economic, and political implications or repercussions. Simple accident: The cloud from a volcano blocks aviation over at least a quarter of the planet. Real catastrophe: An earthquake shakes up not just the ground and the buildings on it but also an entire social, political, and moral situation. The question already raised by the Lisbon earthquake of 1755—itself felt from Morocco to northern Europe—which was at the time called the question of "Providence," this question, subtly renewed by Kiarostami as the question "Does Allah allow that?" posed by a character in his film on the Iranian earthquake of 1990,[2] this question can no longer bear that name. We cannot deny telluric or meteorological forces. Nor can we deny the inextricable tangle of technologies, politics, and economies with the movements of these forces. Rousseau wrote to Voltaire, in 1756, "Concede, for example, that it was hardly nature who assembled twenty-thousand houses of six or seven stories. If the residents of this large city had been more evenly dispersed and housed less densely, the losses would have been fewer or perhaps none at all."[3] Rousseau could imagine the construction of a city planned differently. But today all our efforts of imagination concerning cities, transportation, energy are led inexorably either toward an increase in technological, social, and economic complexity and interdependence or toward the problems and obstacles raised by complexities already in place and the necessities they impose.

The complexity of interdependent systems (ecological or economic, sociopolitico-ideologic, technoscientific, cultural, logical, etc.) and the existing chains of constraints (electricity, gasoline, uranium, all the rare minerals, etc.)—and their implementation (their civilian and military, social and private uses, etc.)—depend on a general interconnection: that of the money by which all these systems function and to which, in the last analysis, they lead back, since any operation of fabrication, exchange, or distribution must lead to profit. This interconnection expresses an economy guided by the production and self-production of wealth, from which streams an incessant production of new conditions, norms, and constraints of life—not by the reproduction of conditions of existence or the extravagant hoarding of vainglorious wealth. The morphing of the second into the first was the product of what we call "capitalism"—that is, as we know, the process engendered by the accumulation of capital destined for profitable investment and not for vainglorious ostentation.

Marx called money a "general equivalent." It is this equivalence that is being discussed here. Not to think about it by itself, but to reflect that the regime of general equivalence henceforth virtually absorbs, well beyond the monetary or financial sphere but thanks to it and with regard to it, all the spheres of existence of humans, and along with them all things that exist.

This absorption involves a close connection between capitalism and technological development as we know it. More precisely, it is the connection of an equivalence and a limitless interchangeability of forces, products, agents or actors, meanings or values—since the value of any value is its equivalence.

Catastrophes are not all of the same gravity, but they all connect with the totality of interdependences that make up general equivalence. What's more, we must not forget to include wars in this interconnection, more particularly all the modern transformations of the concept and practices of war: "partisan" war, guerrilla warfare, "total" war, "world" war, police operations called "wars," and so on—the systematic development of both heavy and light armaments that favor the proliferation of war and its effects on so-called civilian populations as well as on cultures, herds, soil, and so on. Not to ignore economic warfare, which constantly agitates the system of general equivalence from within.

In brief, it is this equivalence that is catastrophic.

We should not conclude from this, however, that capitalism is the evil subject of this work with which it might be obvious what good subject—or what good *subjectivation*, as people like to say today—it should be contrasted with (a "more human" subject, for example, or one that is "more natural" or "more moral," "more spiritual," or anything having to do with a "resurrected culture").[4] We are not opposing or proposing anything. Nor are we offering a solution for energy problems (phasing out nuclear energy, revolutionizing its management, limiting its expansion, etc.). But we are suggesting that the interdependent totality of "civilization" and its "globalization" must be understood as itself dependent on a profound orientation created over several centuries—without conscious decision, without deliberation—by a humanity that is now headed toward a generalized catastrophe, or at least is now capable of one, and hence is summoned less to rectify this orientation (by reforming it, channeling it, or impeding it) than to think about what this strange business [*histoire*] can mean that it has given rise to and consequently, quite simply, the existence of the world or worlds of which humans seem rather earnestly in charge.

Fukushima, in the beginning of the twenty-first century, revives fears and questions that the twentieth had unleashed for the first time on a large scale and that the century before it had manifested, the century that emerged from the two-fold industrial and democratic revolution, the century of the "conquering bourgeoisie."[5] This conquest has changed—into a domination no longer by the "bourgeois" but by the machine they had served and into a dissipation of what seemed to give meaning or value to that conquest. Meaning and value—which Marx called alienated under general equivalence—themselves become catastrophic, following the Greek etymology of *catastrophe,* upheaval, reversal, overturning, collapse.

The dénouement of Greek tragedy in *katastrophē* carried the play both to its extremity and to its resolution—purification, expulsion, conjuration, abreaction, liberation, release, as you choose: The history of interpretations of *catharsis* is endless. But this history is also the history of our obsession: We have never found the meaning of tragedy, supposing there is a meaning to find, and that "meaning" is always what is invented, but is never what is recovered.

We live no longer either in tragic meaning nor in what, with Christianity, was supposed to transport and elevate tragedy to divine salvation. Nor can we take refuge in any sort of Confucian, Taoist, or Buddhist wisdom: Equivalence does not allow it, despite all our good intentions. We are being exposed to a catastrophe of meaning. Let's not hurry to hide this exposure under pink, blue, red, or black silks. Let us remain exposed, and let us think about what is happening [*ce qui nous arrive*] to us: Let us think that it is we who are arriving, or who are leaving.[6]

1

"To philosophize after Fukushima"—that is the mandate I was given for this conference.[1] Its wording inevitably makes me think of Adorno's: "To write poetry after Auschwitz." There are considerable differences between the two. They are not the differences between "philosophy" and "poetry" since we know those two modes or registers of spiritual or symbolic activity share a complex but strong proximity. The differences, of course, are those between "Fukushima" and "Auschwitz." These differences should certainly not be ignored or minimized in any way. They should, however, be correctly understood. I think that is necessary if I want to give the question I was given a conscientious answer.

First of all, we must remember that Auschwitz has already been several times associated with Hiroshima. The outcome of what is called the Second World War, far from being conceived as the conclusion and peace that should mark the end of a war, presents itself rather as a twofold inauguration: of a

9

scheme for annihilating peoples or human groups by means of a systematically developed technological rationality, and a scheme for annihilating entire populations and mutilating their descendants. Each of these projects was supposed to serve the aim of political domination, which is also to say economic and ideological domination. The second of the two was, moreover, linked to the first by the fact that the war of the United States with Japan entrained the one in which America engaged with Nazi Germany and also induced anxious relations with the Soviet Union.

As we know, the Nazi agenda was animated by a racist and mythological ideology that carried to its height a fury of European, Christian origin, that is, anti-Semitism (which was extended in the name of a fanatical "purity" to include the Roma, homosexuals, Communists, and the handicapped). In this respect, the Hitlerian madness was a product of Europe and is markedly different from the dominating ambition nurtured by the United States as a power conceiving of itself as the *novus ordo seclorum*, "the new order of the world," proclaimed by its seal.

The fact remains, however, that Auschwitz and Hiroshima are also two names that reflect—with their immense differences—a transformation that has affected all of civilization: the involvement of technological rationality in the service of goals incommensurable with any goal that had ever been aimed at before, since these goals embodied the necessity for destruction that was not merely inhuman (inhuman cruelty is an old acquaintance in human history), but entirely conceived and calculated expressly for annihilation. This calculation should be understood as excessive and immoderate compared with all the deadly forms of violence that peoples had ever known through their rivalries, their hostilities, their hatreds and revenges. This excess consists not only in a change of scale but first and foremost in a change in nature. For the first time, it is not simply an enemy that is being suppressed: Human lives taken en masse are annihilated in the name of an aim that goes well beyond combat (the victims, after all, are not combatants) to assert a mastery that bends under its power not only lives in great number but the very configuration of peoples, not only lives but "life" in its forms, relationships, generations, and representations. Human life in its capacity to think, create, enjoy, or endure is precipitated into a condition worse than misery itself: a stupor, a distractedness, a horror, a hopeless torpor.

2

What is common to both these names, Auschwitz and Hiroshima, is a crossing of limits—not the limits of morality, or of politics, or of humanity in the sense of a feeling for human dignity, but the limits of existence and of a world where humanity exists, that is, where it can risk sketching out, giving shape to meaning. The significance of these enterprises that overflow from war and crime is in fact every time a significance wholly included within a sphere independent of the existence of the world: the sphere of a projection of possibilities at once fantastical and technological that have their own ends, or more precisely whose ends are openly for their own proliferation, in the exponential growth of figures and powers that have value for and by themselves, indifferent to the existence of the world and of all its beings.

That is why the names of Auschwitz and Hiroshima have become names on the outermost margin of names,

names that name only a kind of de-nomination—of defiguration, decomposition. About these names we must hear what Paul Celan says in a poem that can, for precise reasons, be read just as easily with either of the names in mind:

The place, where they lay, it has
a name—it has
none. They didn't lie there. Something
lay between them. They
didn't see through it.[1]

A proper noun is always a way to pass beyond signification. It signifies itself and nothing else. About the denomination that is that of these two names, we could say that instead of passing beyond, they fall below all signification. They signify an annihilation of meaning.

Here we have now the name of Fukushima. It is accompanied by the sinister privilege that makes it rhyme with Hiroshima. We must of course be wary of letting ourselves be carried away by this rhyme and its rhythm. The philosopher Satoshi Ukai has warned us about this risk in recalling that the name "Fukushima" does not suffice to designate all the regions affected (he names the counties of Miyagi and Iwate); and we must also take into consideration the traditional overexploitation of northeastern Japan by the central government.[2] We must not in fact confuse the name Hiroshima—the target of enemy bombing—with that of Fukushima, a name in which are mingled several orders of natural and technological, political and economic phenomena.

At the same time, it is not possible to ignore what is suggested by the rhyme of these two names, for this rhyme gathers together—reluctantly and against all poetry—the ferment of something shared. It is a question—and since March 11, 2011, we have not stopped chewing on this bitter pill—of nuclear energy itself.

3

As soon as we undertake this bringing together, this continuity, a contradiction seems to arise: The military atom is not the civilian atom; an enemy attack is not a country's electrical grid. It is here that the grating poetry of this vexatious rhyme opens onto philosophy: What can "after Fukushima" mean?

It is a question first of all of what "after" means. Certain "after"s have rather the value of "that which succeeds," that which comes later on: That is the value we have given to the "post" prefix set next to, for instance, "modern" in "post-modern," which designates the "after" of this "modern," which is itself conceived as an incessant "before," as the time that precedes itself, that anticipates its future (we have even known the word *futurism*). But the "after" we are speaking of here stems on the contrary not from succession but from rupture, and less from anticipation than from suspense, even stupor. It is an "after" that means: Is there an after? Is there anything that follows? Are we still headed somewhere?

Where Is Our Future? That is the title of a text the philosopher Osamu Nishitani wrote one month after the tsunami of March 11, 2011. It is a matter of finding out if there is a future. It is possible that there may not be one (or that there may be one that is in its turn catastrophic). It is a matter of orientation [*sens*], direction, path—and at the same time of meaning [*sens*] as signification or value. Nishitani here not only develops a political, social, and economic analysis of the situation but also questions "the civilization of the atom."[1]

To this "after" I want to link the "after" of a poet. Ryoko Sekiguchi lives in Paris but maintains personal and literary ties with Japan. Under the title *Ce n'est pas un hasard* [It is Not a Coincidence] she published the journal she started keeping after the tsunami (starting the day before, March 10, for reasons I'll let you discover in her book).[2] On April 29 she writes: "Forty-nine days after the earthquake. This is the day in Buddhist ritual when they say the soul joins the hereafter definitively." This note has a twofold stress: "they say" marks a distance from the belief mentioned, and "definitively," while reporting the content of the belief, also resounds with something irremediable that no "hereafter" can console.

4

et us start again from what these two testimonies tell us: Civilization, irremediable? Civilization of the irremediable or an irremediable civilization? I think, in fact, that the question of after Fukushima is posed in these terms. They are, moreover, more or less the terms Freud used in speaking of what he called *Das Unbehagen in der Kultur*, that is, less *malaise* or *discontent* in English (although both are correct translations) than *mal-être* (ill-being): Freud sees nothing in these other than the fact that humanity is in a position to destroy itself thanks to our mastery over natural forces.[1] Freud had no idea of atomic energy when he wrote these lines in 1929. The technological methods deployed in the First World War were quite enough to give him a foretaste of what Camus would call, after Hiroshima, the suicidal savagery of civilization.[2]

We might wonder if it is truly a matter of civilization in its entirety, since "civilian" use of the atom is distinguished from its military use. First, we must remember that military technologies are of the same nature as the others—they borrow from and contribute to them many elements. But we must say more and must begin by calling into question the distinction (to say nothing of the contrast) between military and civilian. We know that the concept of war has changed considerably since what were termed "the world wars" and after all the "partisan" wars,[3] wars of colonial liberation, guerrilla warfare, and generally, the involvement of war—armed or else economic, psychological, etc.—in many aspects of our communal existence.

The same Osamu Nishitani could speak, on March 19, 2011, of a state of "war without enemy." A war without enemy is a war against ourselves. The problem posed by the "peaceful" use of the atom is that of its extreme, and extremely lasting, harmfulness. This harmfulness is the same after Hiroshima as after Three Mile Island, Chernobyl, and Fukushima. All this is well known. What remains to be considered, though, goes beyond the range of solutions. For a solution—whether it consists of giving up nuclear energy or of considerably augmenting protective measures—remains caught in the orbit of the totality of technological arrangements and behaviors within which our lives are lived—within which civilization develops. The race for control and for alternative methods remains unaltered on the horizon of a civilization that, for the sake of expediency, I'll call here "progress" and "mastery over nature."

If this civilization turns out to be at the same time a civilization of war against ourselves and against the world, if mastery coils back on itself subjecting us to ever-increasing constraints as we try to escape the previous ones, replacing every kind of progress with an aggravation of our condition, and if what had been the power of the people—the power of their technologies but also of their abilities to resist them—finally sets about exercising an autonomous power over them and over the rest of beings, then we are faced with a task as urgent as the task of making the broken reactors of Fukushima and the substances that have escaped from them powerless to cause harm.

This observation is not new. Perhaps it has even been presented until now only too often in a way that could be described as "pessimistic," using Heidegger's thinking on technology or that of Günther Anders, author of *Hiroshima ist überall* (Hiroshima Is Everywhere) whose title condenses the stern yet too little heeded lesson, too little mentioned in any case in the world of philosophers.[4] But Freud was also called a pessimist, whereas reading his lines from 1929 today quoted above, we are struck rather by their virtue of anticipation.

We should know, though, that visionary or prophetic anticipation does not exist. What after the fact seems prophetic was in fact seen clearly at the time. It is not a question of pessimism but of clear vision. Nor is it a question of repeating, like so many others, that all times and all cultures—at least the ones conceived of as "civilization"—have always deplored the disastrous course of history or else regretted a lost golden age. Our time—as it has been able to see itself at least since the first "world war"—is the era that knows it is capable of an "end of days" that would be a deed created by humans. Günther Anders writes: "Today, since the apocalypse is technically possible and even likely, it stands alone before us: no one believes anymore that a 'kingdom of God' will follow it. Not even the most Christian of Christians."[5]

He could have added that the very meaning of the word *apocalypse* is found to be affected by it. For in Greek it means "unveiling" or "revelation." When a revelation reveals that there is nothing to reveal, it slams shut. Perhaps we could transpose this by speaking of a *satori* that awakens to nothing, to no understanding.

5

hat Fukushima adds to Hiroshima is the threat of an apocalypse that opens onto nothing, onto the negation of the apocalypse itself, a threat that depends not just on military use of the atom and perhaps not even on the sole use of the atom in general. Actually, these uses themselves are part of a larger configuration where the deepest lineaments of our civilization are sketched.

Military use gives us an idea of this configuration. Nuclear weapons have engendered by their power a strategy of dissuasion sometimes hailed as a new condition of peace and often called the "balance of terror." As we know, this balance itself gives rise to the wish to possess nuclear weapons in order to become in turn an agent of this balance, that is, a threat of terror. Of this terror, it should be said in passing, we might inquire what unperceived links it shares with what we call "terrorism," which existed before nuclear weapons. Generally we can say that terror designates an absence or an overvaulting [*outrepassement*] of relationship: It acts by itself, alone; it does not engage a relationship.

In the balance of terror, the relationship between strong and weak, or between powerful and less powerful, does not exist. Nuclear weapons, even of unequal power (if we set aside weapons designated as strictly "tactical"), are capable of acts of destruction the strength of which we cannot conceive. It is the same absolute force that can act in many places at once and that involves both the destruction that occurs in an instant and also the destruction or damage that will affect living beings, water, soil, and all the natural world for a very long time. If the relationship between the strong and the less strong disappears, then there disappear with it the possibilities for calculating or imagining strategies to confront the force. There is no more meaning in notions like "David and Goliath," "Ulysses and the Cyclops," or "Zatoichi: The Blind Swordsman."

Whereas the balance of power [*le rapport des forces*] was a relationship [*rapport*], despite everything, the balance of terror annuls any relationship. It replaces it by what the word *balance* designates: the equivalence that annuls tension by keeping it equal and constant. There is no longer strictly speaking a confrontation; there is no longer strictly speaking any confrontation with the other since it is absolutely the same confronting the same. And its power is such that it can almost no longer be thought of as depending on human wills that are supposed to command its use: A mere mistake or a stroke of madness could set off its use and plunge us into the horror of an unspeakable devastation. It is on the prospect of this devastation that Kubrick's *Dr. Strangelove* ends, the parable of an unbearable possibility. It is no longer just a question of human decision: This decision becomes such that what it decides goes beyond anything calculable as the effects of some decision.

6

*W*ith equivalence and the incalculable we have already extended our perspective beyond nuclear use by the military. In fact, with these two features we can characterize not just the general use of nuclear energy but, even more widely, the nature of the general disposition of force in this world we have given ourselves.

Equivalence means the state of forces that govern themselves in some way by themselves. Whether it is a question of a broken nuclear reactor or a bomb, whether the reactor or the weapon is more or less powerful, the excessiveness of their effects in space and time makes them equal to the excess associated with the means of controlling them and even more of neutralizing them. This is not absolutely new: Coal, electricity, and oil have already brought these problems with them, sufferings or wounds of civilization that exceed the capacities of technical as well as political control. We can, for instance, struggle to advocate for the electric car, but as of now there is no likelihood of its replacing gasoline-powered cars. There is a great likelihood, though, of the exhaustion of petroleum resources.

In every direction we can imagine, whether it's a matter of "perfecting" techniques to control or annul their effects or else abandoning or neutralizing the use of some of them, it seems impossible to envisage anything but ever-increasing forms of interdependence, processes becoming ever more intricate and complex, as many intricacies and complexities as accumulate between material technologies and social, psychological, political techniques. The automobile demanded the seat belt and the airbag, speed limits, increased sanctions for driving under the influence of alcohol and other drugs—witness the invention of a device capable of preventing the car from starting if the driver's breath reveals a certain alcohol level. There is no end to the exponential augmentation of techniques of control with which medical techniques, public health techniques, and so on are (obviously) intertwined.

Medicine is a domain favorable to these developments we could call technical self-generation. Organ transplants, for instance, involve research into immune-suppressive substances whose so-called secondary effects, harmful to the organism, must be combated by other substances that, in turn, cause effects that must be combated, and so on. In this way we produce bodies that are veritable chemical complexes. Similar remarks can be made about cancers and about what we could call the cancer of cancers: the proliferation of varieties of cancer linked to all sorts of causes located in the food industry and other industries.

In all these self-generated and self-complexified structures—or self-complicating, self-obscuring structures—there reigns what I have called equivalence: Forces fight each other and compensate for each other, substitute for each other. Once we have replaced the given, nonproduced forces (the ones we used to call "natural," like wind and muscle) with produced forces (steam, electricity, the atom), we have entered into a general configuration where the forces of production of other forces and the other forces of production or action share a close symbiosis, a generalized interconnection that seems to make inevitable an unlimited development of all forces and all their interactions, retroactions, excitations, attractions, and repulsions that, finally, act as incessant recursions [*renvois*] of the same to the same. From action to reaction, there is no rapport or relation: There is connection, concord and discord, going and coming, but no relation if what we call "relation" always involves the incommensurable, that which makes one in the relationship absolutely not equivalent to the other.

7

The incommensurability of the same and the other cannot be related to the incalculability of what challenges our power to decide. No one can truly calculate the consequences of Fukushima, for humans, for the region, the earth, the streams, and the sea, for the energy economy of Japan, for calling into question, abandoning, or increasing control of nuclear reactors all over the world, and thus for the energy economy worldwide. But all this is incalculable because it challenges the capacities of calculation whereas, at the same time, what we plan or project remains within the order of calculation, even if it is out of our reach.

The incommensurable is of a different nature: It is not even involved in the order of calculation; it opens onto the absolute distance and difference of what is other—not only the other human person but also what is other than human: animal, vegetable, mineral, divine. But by naming these categories, we experience how fragile they are made by technology, which, to take one example, makes animal and vegetable dependent on the synthetic substances with which they are fed, or which exposes soil, plants, and products to spray or radiation (think of ionizing radiation as a technique to preserve food). As for the divine, it is superfluous to insist on the shift it has undergone thanks to these operations. What is turned upside-down is in fact the distribution of substances, characters, and registers through all modes of existence, representation, conception, and imagination. Where there had been for all humankind before us an ordered, configured world, with its systems, its hierarchies, its roles, we see unfurling before us more than a transformation: a generalized transformability that, at the same time, does not provide the unity of some principle or law of transformation, but that on the contrary never ceases diversifying and multiplying the modalities, directions, causalities of all forms of transformation, transport, transposition, or transmutation.

There has arisen in the world, and it is arising *as a world* (just like that *plurality of worlds* contemplated by contemporary physics), a circulation, an interaction, a communication, and information in the strong, intense sense of these words, which place existences in an ever tighter and more networked interrelation and interdependence. A major element of this interconnection is the incalculable in the form of the very large number. The very large number—from which stem both what we call the cosmic "infinitely great" and also the subatomic "infinitely small"—is manifested on the scale of our own experience as the human population (soon to be seven billion as I write these lines) as well as in the quantities of energy consumed, transportation carried out, products made, patents registered, contracts concluded. These large numbers are both effects and agents of this general and increasing interconnection. They are also what multiplies the effects of natural phenomena—independent of the fact that these phenomena can be themselves affected or provoked by technological causes. A hurricane, a tsunami, a drought today may have effects of a magnitude incomparably beyond what they had been just a hundred years ago.

8

ukushima is a powerfully exemplary event because it shows the close and brutal connections between a seismic quake, a dense population, and a nuclear installation (under inadequate management). It is also exemplary of a node of complex relationships between public powers and private management of the installation, not to mention all the other chains of correlation that extend out from that starting point.

We should not think that the conjunction produced in Fukushima is exceptional. It is certainly not so in Japan, but nor is it on the world scale. It is true that an earthquake and a fragile nuclear plant do not often meet, but wherever you manipulate nuclear energy, risks are present whose dimensions are either incalculable or difficult to calculate. These risks are not limited to the nuclear industry—and I think we must, in order best to reflect on our future, go beyond focusing exclusively on the nuclear. We must add to its risks the others linked to all our technologies, whether it's a question of carbon dioxide emissions or depleting various species of fish, whether it's a question of biogenetic and biometric technologies, nanotechnologies or electronic-financial technologies.

It is the interdependent totality of our technologized world—which is specifically a world of human creation and at the same time a world to which virtually all beings are entirely subjected—whose truth we must think about. Two examples eloquently illustrate our interdependence: that of the ever-increasing systems of "radio frequency identification" (RFID) that allow all sorts of locatability, traceability, connection, and control (of which bar codes were a precursor) and that of the determination of an "atomic time" independent of earthly time and necessary for the worldwide synchronization required by the many digital activities of communication, calculation, exchange, and so forth.

There is, however, a technology that gathers into itself in the purest (if we can use that term) state the features of general interconnection, equivalence, and the incalculable. It is the monetary technology from which capitalist civilization has developed—since that is indeed its proper name. By designating money as "general equivalence," Marx uttered more than the principle of mercantile exchange: He uttered the principle of a general reabsorption of all possible values into this value that defines equivalence, exchangeability, or convertibility of all products and all forces of production. The word *value* should not make us think of those idealist entities that were and for some still are "values," those fetishes, reductions of meanings called "homeland" or "honor," "justice" or "family," "man" or *"care."*[1] Meaning here is reduced, since it is fixed in place, registered, represented—and these representations are precisely the reified

31

residue of the loss of meaning that takes place in the endless fluxes of equivalence.

This is the law of our civilization: The incalculable is calculated as general equivalence. This also means that the incalculable is the calculation itself, that of money and at the same time, by a profound solidarity, that of ends and means, that of ends without end, that of producers and products, that of technologies and profits, that of profits and creations, and so on.

In 2011 Jean-Claude Trichet, the outgoing president of the European Central Bank, declared: "The financial sector must change its values."[2] This declaration, which has already been made in a hundred different ways since the start of the great financial upheavals, in this form takes on an aspect of extreme irony. The agents of global financial interconnection have no other value than pure equivalence. To change "values" would put them out of work. But to call for such a change reveals a refusal to consider this simple truth, a refusal combined with a naïve belief in the possibility of a virtuous handling of general equivalence.

9

ow we have come beyond the meaning that Marx gave his phrase. For him, the equivalence of money could be demystified in favor of the living reality of a production whose social truth is the creation of true humanity. That was for him the historical task of capitalism, to lead to its own transcendence.

We are in the midst of another transcendence, which is that of the dissipation of any vision of a "true humanity." The possibility of representing a "total" human, free from alienation, emancipated from all natural, economic, and ideological subjection, has faded away in the very progress of general equivalence becoming the equivalence and interconnection of all goals and all possibilities.

There are now seven billion human beings and millions of billions of other living beings caught in an interdependence where the demarcations between "nature" and "technology" are erased, between the different technologies, between their ends and means, between our existences as ends in themselves and our social lives as endlessly equivalent means to ends: wealth, health, productivity, knowledge, authority, imagination, all enlisted in the same logic whose general principle seems to be the conversion of quantity into quality. Large numbers lay down the law, whether they be of money, population, speed, power, circulation, information, and so on. In any case, and in the interconnection of all these registers, "quality," that is, "value" or "meaning," is dispersed in the interactive correlation of all large numbers. What we have for almost two centuries called "nihilism" is the exact opposite of what we had hoped to achieve by technology, mastery over fate. Communication becomes contamination; transmission becomes contagion.

That is what makes Fukushima exemplary: An earthquake and the tsunami it caused become a technological catastrophe, which itself becomes a social, economic, political, and finally philosophical earthquake, at the same time as this series intersects or intertwines with the series of financial catastrophes, of their effects on Europe in particular and of the repercussions of these effects on all global relationships.

There are no more natural catastrophes: There is only a civilizational catastrophe that expands every time. This can be demonstrated with each so-called natural catastrophe— earthquake, flood, or volcanic eruption—to say nothing of the upheavals produced in nature by our technologies.

We have, in fact, transformed nature, and we can no longer speak of it. We must attempt to think of a totality in which the distinction between nature and technology is no longer valid and in which, at the same time, a relationship of "this world" to any "other world" is also no longer valid.

This condition imposed on our thinking surpasses greatly what we sometimes call "a crisis of civilization." This is not a crisis we can cure by means of this same civilization. This condition also goes beyond what is sometimes called a "change of civilization": We do not decide on such a change; we cannot aim for it since we cannot outline the goal to be reached.

Our thinking must no longer be either about crisis or plan. But we know no other model for thinking about the "better." Ever since we have wanted a "better," ever since we have wanted to change and ameliorate the world and humankind, we have only thought in terms of regeneration or new generation: Remake or make a better world and humankind. That, of course, began with the great historical configuration marked by Buddhism, Confucianism, Hellenism, and Western monotheism, which is also the configuration marked by the end of strictly sacrificial (self-sacrificial) relations of human beings with a world of gods. The divine, if it still has not disappeared everywhere, has profoundly changed its meaning. It has also passed, in the West, into the divinization of humanity (called "atheism").

But this divinization has given way, in turn, since "humanism" has not been able to conceive of "the essential worth of the human being,"[1] or of that of "nature," or of that of the "world," or finally that of existence in general. It has given way to an interconnection, to a kind of generalized environmentalism in which everything is environed, is enveloped, and develops according to the reticulation of what has been called an *unconscious technology*[2]—"unconscious" meaning above all, here as well as elsewhere, the tangled web of all beings. This web, this profuse contextualization that has

35

promoted in our modernity the motif of "immanence"—of an adherence to self without "self" in a way—gives rise to legitimate questionings, suspicions, and doubts that, after God, center on "subject," "meaning," "identity," "symbol."

It does not follow, however, that this immanence and its intricacy should be considered as degradation or degeneration of our past transcendences. We must think in terms other than regeneration or new generation. This should at least begin with a renewed understanding of what "technology" means. Since it is no longer enough to contrast it or pair it with a supposed "nature," we must think—even at fresh expense—of what Heidegger called "the last farewell of being." That means at least this: Technology is not an assembly of functioning means; it is the mode of our existence. This mode exposes us to a condition of finality that had till now been unheard-of: Everything becomes the end and the means of everything. In one sense, there are no more ends or means. General equivalence has this meaning too, an equivocal meaning. In the mutual cross-referencing [*renvoi*] of everything are also at play both the destruction of all construction and what I might call *struction,* in the sense of heaping up [*amoncellement*] without putting together [*assemblage*].[3]

What assembling could we invent? How can we assemble the pieces of a world, of various worlds, of existences that cross through them? How can we assemble ourselves, "us," all beings? Fukushima can make us decide not to use nuclear energy anymore or to use it differently: I cannot enter here into the considerations these options involve. I can instead assert that no option will make us emerge from the endless equivalence of ends and means if we do not emerge from finality itself—from aiming, from planning, and projecting a future in general. That our ends have become future ends, that will be the main product of what we call the West or more generally the "modern." To speak of "postmodern" is correct if we mean by that giving up any aim for a future conceived of as the unity of a meaning to come. But it is not enough, since that remains trapped in a scheme of succession, of before and after.

What would be decisive, then, would be to think in the present and to think the present.[4] No longer the end of ends to come, or even a felicitous anarchic dispersion of ends, but the present as the element of the near-at-hand. The end is always far away; the present is the place of closeness—with the world, others, oneself. If we want to speak of "end," we must say that the present has its end in itself—like technology, in short, but without the addition of "final" representations. The present has its end in itself in both senses of the word *end*: its goal and its cessation. Finality and finitude joined together—which means, if we think about it, opening onto the infinite. Knowledge of existence as infinite capacity for meaning. Thinking about "meaning" as not an end to reach, but that which is possible to be close to. Fukushima forbids all present: It is the collapse of future goals that forces us to work with other futures. Let us try in fact to work with other futures—but under the condition of the ever-renewed present.

10

The present I evoke thus is not the present of the immediate, that of the pure and simple inert position where reason and desire are fixed in stupor or in repletion, without past or future, nor is it one of the fleeting or lightning-quick instant of decision, that exemplary decision made by the trader who shifts millions from one account to another: This present is one in which we are escaping toward a future that we desire and that we want to ignore at the same time (which does not prevent us from escaping also toward a past of nostalgia or the collection of antiques). I am speaking of a present in which something or someone presents itself: the present of an arrival, an approach. That is the exact opposite of general equivalence—which is also that of all chronologic presents that follow each other and that must be counted. The opposite is the nonequivalence of all singularities: those of persons and moments, places, gestures of a person, those of the hours of the day or night, those of words spoken, those of clouds that pass, plants that grow with a knowing slowness. This nonequivalence exists by the attention brought to these singularities—to a color, to a sound, to a smell. The contemplation of cherry trees in flower, that ceremony called *hanami* in Japanese and that is rightly famous throughout the world,[1] or else a glance at the brilliance of a precious stone—whose "price" is not its cost—as well as the final sonority of *Nun* by Helmut Lachenmann, whose title means "now"—a sonority that is that of the *k* in the word *Musik*.

Each time it is a question of a particular consideration, of attention and tension, of respect, even of what we can go so far as to call adoration, directed at singularity as such. It is not that "respect for nature" advocated by facile ecologist discourse or a "respect for human rights" as advocated by another often ignored discourse—ignored even though the respects in question are not to be scorned—it is not that, then, but rather an esteem in the most intense sense of the word: a sense that turns its back on "valuation" measures. For estimation—or valuation—belongs to the series of calculations of general equivalence, whether it be of money or its substitutes, which are the equivalence of forces, capacities, individuals, risks, speeds, and so on. Esteem on the contrary summons the singular and its singular way to come into presence—flower, face, or tone.

Esteem, once and for all, goes beyond itself and addresses something inestimable, a term used in French to designate something more precious than any price, something incalculable, so exceeding any possible calculation that one does not even try to imagine it.

The present I mean to evoke is one that opens to this esteem of the singular and turns away from general equivalence and from its evaluation of past and future times, from the accumulation of antiquities and construction of projects. No culture has lived as our modern culture has in the endless accumulation of archives and expectations. No culture has made present the past and the future to the point of removing the present from its own passage. All other cultures, on the contrary, have known how to care for the approach of singular presence.

It is true that most of these cultures have also supported tyrannies, cruelties, slaveries, anguishes whose abolition modern culture has willed. But it has come to experience itself as tyranny, cruelty, slavery, and anguish. It is up to us, after Fukushima, to open other paths, whether they be inside or outside this culture that is drowning itself.

To begin, we must understand that equivalence is not equality. It is not the equality that the French Republic sets between liberty and fraternity and that can in fact be thought of as both a synthesis and a surpassing of those two notions. Equality designates here the strict equality in dignity of all living humans[2]—not excluding other registers of dignity for all living beings, even for all things. Dignity is the name of the value that is absolutely valid (*Würde* is the German Kant uses, from the same family as *Wert*, value). It means it has no "worth" if "to have worth" [*valoir*] implies a scale of measure; it is thus *priceless,* as we say to mean *inestimable* and thus *incommensurable*. Equality is not that equivalence of individuals of which the idea of "democracy" makes us think first of all—favoring thus insidiously both mercantile equivalence and the atomization of "subjects," each as catastrophic as the other. Quite the opposite, "democracy" should be thought of starting only from the equality of incommensurables: absolute and irreducible singulars that are not individuals or social groups but sudden appearances, arrivals and departures, voices, tones—here and now, every instant.

To demand equality for tomorrow is first of all to assert it today, and by the same gesture to reject catastrophic equivalence. It is to assert common equality, common incommensurability: a communism of nonequivalence.

Questions for Jean-Luc Nancy

YUJI NISHIYAMA AND YOTETSU TONAKI, SEPTEMBER 2013

Y.N. AND Y.T.: The Japanese translation of your book *After Fukushima* had quite an impact on Japan, since it's the first sincere, valuable response by a foreign philosopher to Fukushima. After the catastrophe in Fukushima, your book revealed from a broad perspective a philosophical reflection on the configuration of capitalism and technology (you once called it *écotechnie*, "ecotechnology") which produced a serious catastrophe in our civilization.

Allow me to ask one of the questions missing from your thinking: It's the question of the victim, or the work of mourning after the catastrophe. The characteristic of catastrophe is a large number of victims (dead, disappeared, refugees, etc.); there remains the question of responsibility to these victims.

In your conclusion, you remarked on "a present in which something or someone presents itself: the present of an arrival, an approach." Here it's a question of "a particular consideration, of attention and tension, of respect, even of what we can go so far as to call adoration, directed at singularity as such" in order to turn away from general equivalence.

QUESTIONS FOR JEAN-LUC NANCY

My question is: Does the question of responsibility to
the victims also provide a singular opportunity to deny
catastrophic equivalence, to assert a "communism of nonequivalence"?

J.-L.N.: Yes, without a doubt. For what we owe victims,
beyond practical aid and basic care, is to show them that we
know what they are victims of—even if it is harder to know
that one is the victim of an entire system and not just a few
"evil" individuals—even less of a "natural" catastrophe.
Victims are victims in that they are treated as equivalent
objects by a system that refuses to calculate certain risks
because it calculates only by short-term productivity.

Y.N. AND Y.T.: In 1991, during the Gulf War, you wrote an
article called "War, Law, Sovereignty—Technē." Noting
that the possibility of war is indissociable from the notion of
sovereignty, you write, "War is sovereignty's technology par
excellence; it is its setting to work and its supreme execution
(end)."[1] To paraphrase your expression, nuclear energy is
also "sovereignty's technology par excellence; it is its setting
to work [mise en oeuvre] and its supreme execution (end)" in
our civilization. For nuclear technology is a singular technology that is quite different from other modern energies
(fossil-fuel energies: natural gas, coal, oil), in the aim of exe-
cuting (ex-sequor: following to the end) phusis and technē in
this new configuration.

In these conditions, nuclear technology concerns the
notion of sovereignty in the twentieth century. Usually, the
sovereign state must in fact ensure energy independence.
This tendency has been remarkable in France as well as in

Japan since the 1960s. In these historical contexts, nuclear technology (we can call it "sovereign technology") formed networks of political, economic, and cultural power in these two countries.

What do you think about the connection between technology and sovereignty in the nuclear age?

J.-L.N.: For a number of reasons—where technology plays a determining role—sovereignty is outdated in the present situation: The state can no longer be determined by its territory or its population, and it can no longer be regarded as independent of those economic powers whose extension and powers are global (it has never been completely independent, but from now on its dependency surpasses its independence). That is why at this time a great geopolitical realignment is occurring, whereby Europe and North America are becoming secondary compared to the Pacific countries and to Brazil. It is possible that this shift might change nothing in the eco-techno-political functioning. But since it is accompanied by these interdependences we've just mentioned, it is also possible that it will require new definitions of "states," of "international law," etc.

But even that is not the most important thing: What is fundamental is the very motive for "economic growth" and hence of technology conceived and managed from that perspective. Yet we can oppose nothing to "growth" unless we conceive of another civilization, a new sense of existence not enslaved to production but freed for itself. Which implies that this "for itself" finds its own meaning, the meaning of its "own" fact of being.

Y.N. AND Y.T.: Exactly two and a half years after the nuclear accident in Fukushima, we are witnessing in Japan, along with a number of laudable reconstruction efforts, a more or less general "forgetting." Especially in the province of Fukushima, where some places are still contaminated, even outside the forbidden zones, its two million inhabitants are not merely encouraged to forget, but they themselves are trying to forget the tragic past and the no less painful present. The same is true for those who live far from that region. Yet this forgetting does not seem to me to stem from a lack or defect of sensibility, but is an integral part of the process of catastrophe-reconstruction: We must forget and hide in order to restore the normal or everyday nature of life and, if possible, to make it better than before. Just as if, unlike the catastrophic explosion that exposes and unveils what had been enclosed and hidden (for instance, the radioactivity enclosed in the reactor), we had on the contrary to forget or "bury" the very fact of this exposure. (What is at stake in this problem consists, I think, not just of the unveiling/enclosing relationship as such, but above all the forgetting that is a part of the very process which imposes [re]normalization). What do you think of this kind of "forgetting"?

J.-L.N.: Forgetting is essential to life. It's an extraordinary force. You just have to know what you should be forgetting: catastrophe itself, its unhappiness, its suffering—but if you forget its causes and at the same time also its consequences, that's something else! But that isn't always something we "forget"—often we've never really thought about it at all.

QUESTIONS FOR JEAN-LUC NANCY

Y.N. AND Y.T.: I would like to ask you to clarify a little what you call "communism" at the end of your book *After Fukushima: The Equivalence of Catastrophes*. It seems to me that you are evoking not just a theoretical modality of being with (or of appearing with, *comparution*), but also an outline of a "practical" modality of being communally shared by singular beings, nonequivalent and hence incommensurable. It's a question of a presence of those who resist not only all common measure, but also all actualization or *mise en oeuvre*, a presence that could not easily be "represented," by introducing it, for instance, into the already settled regime of representative democracy. From this communism of informals, so to speak, what "form" can we extract to think about a "democracy to come"? In other words, how can we make ourselves "manifest"? What sort of communication (Twitter, Facebook . . .) is possible in the interaction of nonequivalents? Finally, what thinking about "praxis" or "doing" is possible in this concept of communism of nonequivalents (I'm thinking not just of a chapter called precisely "Praxis" in your book *The Truth of Democracy*, but also of the lecture you gave in March 2012 at the Société française de philosophie titled "Que Faire?"[2]

J.-L.N.: I am not able or willing to outline a kind of schema of society or politics. It's pointless to play at being the architects of the future: Let's let the future do that and open up possibilities. But the fact remains that the most common communication, if I dare say it, is always and constantly at our disposal. By internet, yes, but I'm less sensitive to so-called "social" networks (a revealing expression) than to the possibilities of speaking with each other and seeing each other (Skype, for instance), but more precisely to the circulation of thoughts, words, writings, images, visual and musical forms, of daily life, to all this circulation that makes a still unknown sense, not yet even "sensed," so to speak, but that will not fail to make sense, in the long run. For we continue to live very modestly, every day, as we live—as one lives not in the sense that Heidegger writes about in *Sein und Zeit* but in the sense where in the same book he says that "the authentic is nothing but the modified grasp of the inauthentic," a statement that he does not develop but that no doubt we ourselves are just beginning to develop.

"Communism" is first of all all of us, we who live in common, we who have more and more common givens in life—this computer for instance, this instant circulation of letters between Tokyo and Strasbourg (or perhaps you're not in Tokyo?). More and more everyday "common" things, ordinary and hence more and more motives and reasons to discern what is incomparable and nonequivalent among "us."

It's a Catastrophe!

Interview with Jean-Luc Nancy

DANIELLE COHEN-LEVINAS

D.C.-L.: In a book you called *After Fukushima: The Equivalence of Catastrophes*, which you wrote in 2012, after the Fukushima catastrophe, you write:

> The "equivalence" of catastrophes here means to assert that the spread or proliferation of repercussions from every kind of disaster hereafter will bear the mark of the paradigm represented by nuclear risk.

In other words, the effects of a catastrophe are henceforth to be thought of in terms of interconnection, or the "symbiosis of technologies" (your words). It is a question, then, of catastrophic equivalence, in the literal sense of the word.

Does this equivalence, which includes wars—nuclear, economic, political, spiritual—amount to an equivalence in the very meaning of the world, of history, of humanity?

J.-L.N.: We should emphasize first that equivalence is at play between catastrophes we usually call "natural" (so that the word "catastrophes" commonly implies just this aspect, although when we say "natural" we're really thinking of human catastrophes) and precisely these human catastrophes—wars, massacres, destruction of all kinds. Equivalence stems first from the fact that there's not much we can term simply "natural," since the ravages of a tsunami or a hurricane are immediately multiplied on the human scale, and more than that, they modify and are modified by industry, urbanism, politics, etc. Rousseau long ago noted that there was nothing "natural" about the height of the buildings in Lisbon. . . . What can we say about a nuclear power plant by the sea, one maintained in a defective condition?

But how should we understand your extrapolation toward an "equivalence in the very meaning of the world, of history, of humanity"? You don't use the plural, but I understand it as: equivalence of all meanings, histories, peoples. That is called "nihilism." Nihilism is catastrophe. But it's from within that we can emerge from this, as Nietzsche saw. How can we make equivalence into a possibility for nonequivalence, that is, a difference in value (or in meaning: value and meaning are at bottom the same notion)? Democracy calls for the equality of everyone. Is that an equivalence? In the eyes of law and ethics, yes. But in terms of the labor economy this equivalence lends itself to all manner of inequalities, to the wildest variability of wages, to systematized unemployment. . . . As soon as we speak of the equality of wages, we anger those who argue that natural equality places people on equal footing in a market that treats them all equivalently by rewarding them in a very unequal way.

Added to this—or else implied in this—is the fact that wealth itself is that of the equivalence of currency, which finally measures (it's worth noting) what in itself is nonequivalent (works of art, human lives, health, even technological inventions). Hoarding wealth and pomp (jewelry, ornaments of every kind) is tendentiously confused with the wealth of investment and production (owning the means of production).

D.C.-L.: I've titled this interview with you "It's a Catastrophe!" Like an observation, an exclamation in the midst of the generalized disaster which forces us to shift the question of catastrophe elsewhere, somewhere away from our classic reference points in the Greek sense of the word. We have always thought in terms of healing catastrophes, or restoration. But now? How can we think about what doesn't stop being catastrophic?

J.-L.N.: It's a very delicate question, since we should also emphasize that "it's a catastrophe!"—you chose the right expression!—is a cry or a complaint that resounds periodically. The Romans shouted it at the end of the Empire, and the people who experienced the Thirty Years' War, as well as those who took part in the Fronde rebellion in France, Native Americans faced with the conquistadors, Southerners at the end of the Civil War, European Catholics at the end of the nineteenth century, and so on—to use only a few examples chosen at random. Still, the twentieth century seems to have been one of generalized catastrophe—the global expansion of what we call capitalism, and which is nothing but the totality—capitalist/ democratic/ technocratic—of a civilization or (more precisely) of a de-civilization. This civilization began to doubt itself, both practically and philosophically: It became a generalized war between entities that had long stopped being the Sovereign States of long ago but that became economic-ideological complexes of power arguing over a global market of merchandise both material and symbolic ("communication," "media," etc.).

But civilizations are mortal—that's a phrase that Europe may not have invented (Plato saw clearly that Egypt had lost its splendor) but that it announced in the twentieth century as a discovery, and received it with a certain anguish from which it has not really recovered. What's new is a civilization that does not know how it is different from previous civilizations, or that does not have a more or less clear awareness of the presence of any other cultures (the case no doubt for all cultures till now). That there are today obvious differences between regions in the world does not prevent there being everywhere the same "economic, technological and partially at least ideological" forms that prevail (I say "partially" for the last term since there are regions where religions or collective mentalities clearly stray from the norm; but everything shows that the norms nevertheless operate indirectly).

Catastrophe, that is, the turning-back, overturning, and ruin according to the Greek sense of the word, seems to consist of this civilization turning back and falling over itself, making progress into a blind race, "humanity" an ever more unsettling enigma, and meaning a utilitarian infinity instead of an infinity of adoration.

D.C.-L.: I noted this phrase in your book, which held my attention and intrigued me:

Let us start again from what these two testimonies tell us: Civilization, irremediable? Civilization of the irremediable or an irremediable civilization? I think, in fact, that the question of after Fukushima is posed in these terms.

Does that mean for you that before, before Fukushima, our civilization did not experience the irremediable, or was not itself an irremediable civilization? Hasn't our civilization always identified itself by the fact that it was and is a civilization of war, determined by war and determining it?

J.-L.N.: Of war, I don't think so, since I don't see any society or culture exempt from war. War itself, as legitimate, even sacred, conflict, between collective entities ("states" or whatever you'd like to call them), has disappeared with our culture. It has become confrontation without limits (or else formal and always violated) of techno-economic powers. The effects of classic war were in principle remediable—first of all one could "make peace." Whatever the case with pacts and treatises, that was there in principle. Today's destructions are such they cannot be repaired: We can only replace, or else rather substitute. Think about the cities rebuilt after the end of wars: They're other cities, which can on occasion become monuments of a new architecture (I'm thinking of Le Havre), proving that war does indeed lead to operations that are technological, urbanistic, even aesthetic, and of course economic.

What's more, it's well known that military technologies are at the forefront of a number of developments in several fields. But it should be added that technological developments are at the forefront of formidable economic and social conflicts: Conquering a market requires strategy, tactics, engagement, etc., . . . yet we have reached a point where it is very hard to represent ourselves as exempt from these conflicts and their motives. . . . The result of this is the irremediable, or any case the irreversible.

"Irreparable" implies both the vision of an integral state toward which a "reparation" could at least roughly tend, a *restitutio ad integrum*, and the realization that such a state is out of our reach, even roughly or in a legislated way—and that, on the other hand, there is no indication of what should be substituted for the destroyed or disappeared. I always refer to my favorite comparison: The sixth-century Romans saw everything carried away in a limitless *inclinatio* to which they could see no opposing principle; the Christians among them expected an apocalypse; the Jews, however, remained in the present, which is characteristic of them, and which at that era did not yet earn them the hatred of the Christians, who had not yet entered history.

History, actually, is the first manifestation of catastrophe: procedure, growth, plan, then progress. Already Rome bore an aim that can be described as "historic," and already that aim collapsed under Rome's own sway.

D.C.-L.: Haven't we ourselves become the products of this equivalence? In your book you quote Heidegger's *Letter on Humanism*, recalling that humanism was incapable of thinking about the grandeur of the human or of the world, even less the grandeur of "existing." When it comes down to it, you are starting from this question: "How can we assemble ourselves, 'us,' all beings?" Is there still a "world" where an "us" is possible? Should we work on other "worlds," as you invite us to do for "other futures": "Let us try in fact to work with other futures—but under the condition of the ever-renewed present."

J.-L.N.: This "let us try in fact" is a concession to the ideology we all share: We must try to make other tomorrows possible. Before, they had to be ones that sang; today we would settle for their not shouting or weeping. But the general scheme of "creating a future" is sick unto death, while at the same time the urgency of managing, designing the future has never been so obvious.

That is why the important thing for me is this "condition of an ever-renewed present," a present I go on to explain this way: I mean not an immobile present but a present within historical mobility, a living sense of each moment, each life, each *hic et nunc* [here and now]. A sense that is characterized by exposure to its own infinity, to its incompleteness [*inachèvement*], a sense that, dare I say, suffices by its very insufficiency—instead of the search for *logos* that always wants a *sufficient reason*.

Before, I evoked a "Jewish present": I know it can have its fixed [*immobiliste*], ritualistic, repetitive version; but it has also been able to give rise to a Spinozan present, one in which one "feels and experiences being eternal," or else a Christian present, one for which it is not a question of waiting for the Parousia but of understanding it as here in this very place, and of knowing that the Messiah has already come, that is, that He is not still to come.

D.C.-L.: Your book ends with a phrase that cannot leave us indifferent. You call for the immeasurable, for "a communism of nonequivalence."

Isn't there a little provocation in this paradoxical phrase? You're touching here on the undeconstructable, the concepts of equality, justice, even democracy.

When catastrophe strikes men, women, children, houses, flowers, world, etc., as was the case with Fukushima, when catastrophe deconstructs even the tiniest atom, what can we make of nonequivalence? Isn't it more a question of a simple dialectical movement of reversal: an equivalence that reverses into nonequivalence?

J.-L.N.: In speaking of nondeconstructable justice, you are referring to Derrida. But I'm not sure if he described equality or democracy in the same way—I'd even say "far from that" if I had texts to back me up, but no matter: Justice as motive for what is absolutely due to the absolute unicity of all existence offers a way of thinking for which, first of all, no received notion of "justice" suffices, and for which, secondly, "equality" and "democracy" are notions even less obvious.

On the contrary: Democratic equality forms a kind of presentable face to the reverse side of equivalence. All are equal, since all are worth their force of labor, or even nonlabor, being paid (poorly) not to work where their force would be too costly compared to others. All have "human rights" in which it is almost impossible to find an example that isn't marred by inequality (economic, social, symbolic).

Nonequivalence does not overturn equivalence; it makes it explicit. It says: All are equal in that no one is identical or commensurable with others.

Notes

Preamble

1. This Indian city was the site, on December 3, 1984, of a very serious accident in a pesticide factory, which seriously polluted the region for a long time afterward.

2. *Zendegi va digar hich*—in English, *Life, and Nothing More,* 1991.

3. Jean-Jacques Rousseau, Letter from Rousseau to Voltaire, August 18, 1756, in *Correspondance complète de Jean-Jacques Rousseau*, ed. J. A. Leigh (Geneva, 1967), 4:37–50; translated by R. Spang: http://www .indiana.edu/~enltnmt/texts/JJR%20letter.html.

4. Adorno uses this expression, and explains it as "a culture that was rehashing its traditional values of truth, beauty and goodness as if nothing had happened" (Theodor Adorno, *Metaphysics: Concept and Problems,* trans. Edmund Jephcott [Palo Alto: Stanford University Press, 2002], 119).

5. According to the title of the book by Charles Morazé, *Les Bourgeois conquérants, XIXe siècle* (Paris: Armand Colin, 1957).

6. Thinking about catastrophe or catastrophes already, remarkably and painfully, has its "tradition," which stems at least from Hannah Arendt and Günther Anders, and which Paul Virilio ardently pursues, along with many others. I do not claim to add anything or even to join a

continuity: I am content to punctuate the present moment. What's more, books on catastrophe or catastrophes—or *disasters*, in English—have become very numerous. Thus Annie Le Brun, recently republishing a 1989 text on the subject, can write: "Only twenty or so years had to pass for reflections on catastrophe, ever more specialized, to become almost a genre in itself, ranging from lament to how-to manual" (*Perspective dépravée* [Paris: Éditions du Sandre, 2011], 7). We will try to avoid lament as well as manual, complaint, and fascination, and above all the suspension of thought.

1

1. Videoconference by invitation, in December 2011, of the International Research Center for Philosophy at Tokyo University.

2

1. Paul Celan, "Stretto," in *Paul Celan: Selections,* ed. Pierre Joris, trans. Robert Kelly (Berkeley: University of California Press, 2005), 68.

2. Speech by Satoshi Ukai at the "Nuits du 4 août" 2011 in Peyrelevade, France.

3

1. Text sent in French by its author. The Japanese text is published in *Gendai-Shiso* 39, no. 7 (Tokyo: Seidosha, May 2011): 34–37.

2. Ryoko Sekiguchi, *Ce n'est pas un hasard* (Paris: POL, 2011).

4

1. "The fateful question for the human species seems to me to be whether and to what extent their cultural development will succeed in mastering the disturbance of their communal life by the human instinct of aggression and self-destruction. It may be that in this respect precisely the present time deserves a special interest. Men have gained control over the forces of nature to such an extent that with their help they would have no difficulty in exterminating one another to the last man." Sigmund Freud, *Civilization and Its Discontents*, trans. James Strachey (New York: W. W. Norton, 1961), 92. ("*Die Schicksalsfrage der Menschenart scheint mir*

zu sein, ob und in welchem Maße es ihrer Kulturentwicklung gelingen wird, der Störung des Zusammenlebens durch den menschlichen Aggressions- und Selbstvernichtungstrieb Herr zu warden. In diesem Bezug verdient vielleicht gerade die gegenwärtige Zeit ein besonderes Interesse. Die Menschen haben es jetzt in der Beherrschung der Naturkräfte so weit gebracht, daß sie es mit deren Hilfe leicht haben, einander bis auf den letzten Mann auszurotten."
"Das Unbehagen in der Kultur," in *Gesammelte Werke* [London: Imago, 1972], 14:506.)

2. Albert Camus, in his editorial in *Combat* on August 8, 1945.

3. Term used by Carl Schmitt.

4. Günther Anders, *Hiroshima ist überall: Tagebuch aus Hiroshima und Nagasaki* [*Hiroshima Is Everywhere: Diary from Hiroshima and Nagasaki*] (Munich: C. H. Beck Verlag, 1995).

5. G. Anders, *Le Temps de la fin* (Paris: L'Herne, 2007), 115.

8

1. In English in original.—Trans.

2. Interview with Jean-Claude Trichet in *Le Monde*, October 29, 2011.

9

1. Martin Heidegger, "Letter on 'Humanism'" (1949), trans. Frank A. Capuzzi, http://archive.org/details/HeideggerLetterOnhumanism1949.

2. Cf. Erich Hörl, "Die technologische Bedingung," introduction to the volume of the same name (Berlin: Suhrkamp, 2011), 28. We should, moreover, engage in questioning what is comprised by "science" (assuming we agree that this word can be used in the singular), what is ascribable to "technology," and in what respects it is or is not necessary to pair one with the other.

3. Cf. "De la struction," in Aurélien Barrau and Jean-Luc Nancy, *Dans quels mondes vivons-nous?* (Paris: Galilée, 2011), The German version was published in *Die technologische Bedingung,* ed. Hörl. *Struction* represents in a way the final state of a *deconstruction* whose philosophical necessity it makes us more aware of, beyond the frivolous responses it has received.

4. You might tell me that from this point on I am equivocating with the question of solutions, hence also with the problems that have been set, and that I am escaping into idealism. But idealist solutions are still solutions. It is a question, however, of something other than the "problem-solution" dyad. It is a question of answering a question: Do you want a civilization again? And do you want it to be worthy of that name? Problems and solutions can arise only from the culture where they are born. But the question we are receiving comes from elsewhere and goes further. It involves thinking above all, much more than "solutions." It involves a thinking that, from now on, welcomes the remote. Perhaps another civilization is already here, among us. All the same, that absolutely does not spare us from watching out for the future, from protecting it and letting it occur, by progression or by transformation, by irruption or by revolution, by injunction or by affirmation—all forms whose mingling produces the opposite of a catastrophe.

10

1. A little while after I wrote these lines, I come across Haruki Murakami's speech when he received the International Prize of Catalonia in June 2011. Speaking of Fukushima, he referred to the Japanese culture of the ephemeral—"we cherish the cherry blossoms of spring, the fireflies of summer and the red leaves of autumn"—to contrast with the irremediable destruction "of ethics and values" (Planting Seeds Together: Collaborative Translation initiative inspired by Haruki Murakami's Catalunya International Prize speech on the senri no michi website: http://www.senrinomichi.com/?p=2728).

2. Or the *égaliberté* of Étienne Balibar.

Questions for Jean-Luc Nancy

1. Jean-Luc Nancy, "War, Law, Sovereignty—Technē," in *Being Singular Plural*, trans. Robert Richardson and Anne O'Byrne (Stanford: Stanford University Press, 2000), 117.

2. http://www.sofrphilo.fr/?idPage=12&page=conference&numPage=1&idConference=39